The Adventures Of A Diner Poet

A Mack Capped Romp Through The Canadian Dinerscape

By Jaybo Russell

The Adventures Of A Diner Poet

A Mack Capped Romp Through The Canadian Dinerscape

By Jaybo Russell

For information, please contact Jaybo Russell at

Box 696
Rosebud, AB T0J 2T0

Email: jayborussell@gmail.com
Web address: www.jayborussell.weebly.com

ISBN 978-0-9948736-0-6

For Chelsea. You've become who you really are.

For Mary. You're living the dream.

I'm proud of you both.

"Love is better than anger. Hope is better than fear. Optimism is better than despair. So let us be loving, hopeful, and optimistic. And we'll change the world."

-Jack Layton

About Me

My love of a good story comes from my family. My grandmother hooked me on tales of her uncle - who at age 17, ventured alone from the farm in South Dakota to the goldfields of the Yukon in hopes of striking it rich.

I was mesmerized when my mother talked nostalgically of her adventures as a cook aboard the Uranium Trader, a riverboat plying the mighty Athabasca.

My first attempt at storytelling was in the second grade. I wrote a dramatic short story about Fort Whoop-Up, located in Indian Battle Park near Lethbridge, Alberta. In the Mowat-esque tradition, my narrative was rife with heart-stopping adventure - and some gratuitous mouse eating.

In junior high school, I was a brooding poet and actor. Fortunately for the world, a girlfriend's father mistakenly burnt my poetry collection in a tragic kindling accident.

I kept busy in high school by playing rugby, but found enough time to write and produce my own plays. Unfortunately, people watched my plays - righteously indignant stuff about the injustices in the world. I somehow managed to win a few awards though.

University was an age of discovery for me. My poetry improved, thankfully, and I won some more awards. I wrote countless articles for the University of Lethbridge's *The Meliorist* - a weekly newspaper that attracted many talented folk. It was here I created many lifelong friendships, and polished my writing chops.

I have since written everything from short magazine articles to in-depth research-based historical nonfiction. I'm currently working on a social history of Drumheller, Alberta titled *Of Mines and Men - The Unmentionable History of Drumheller Valley*.

The universe has taught me countless things. One is that the learning never stops. Another is that a positive attitude attracts positive results.

When I'm not busy writing and exploring, I can be found restoring a vintage bicycle, or working under one of my vintage Volkswagen buses.

An Introduction to Diner Poetry

Like a good journalist, a diner poet actively seeks an
engaging story. But instead of creating cynical narratives
filled with grim statistics from leading experts, a diner
poet gleans the thoughts of regular folk - the kind who
frequent the cafes, truck stops, and doughnut shops of
the nation.

Whatever is on their minds becomes the canvas for diner
poetry. Relationships, faith, politics, dreams, history, and
even the Constitution are fair game. God often shows up
in Diner Poetry, by reaching down to stir the pot of our
corporate slavery or our narrow provincialism.

Filled with political insinuation and historic references,
the rhythms of Diner Poetry often skips and dances –
breathes – and then gallops.

Every prairie sunset
I send you wild flowers
And sweetgrass
In my mind.

Every simple night
I sing to you
Serendipitous serenades
Under my breath.

In every lucid dream
I write unread poetry
About you and I laying
Among the tipi rings.

We watch the aurora borealis
Massage our imaginations.
We talk about how we knew
Everything will become one.

As the fiery morning sun
Warms my face
It exposes my
Loneliness under the big sky.

Then I wonder aloud
If my name is really on
The tip of your tongue
Or an echo in the Chinook wind.

Almighty Voice

The Wind played with her hair
Like hastily chosen words
And pushed all the clouds aside
For her.

She stood on a tightrope
Made of a Methodist piano string
Which tickled the air,
Humming at every
Encouraging breeze.

She glanced down
To view the stubborn province far below.
"Soften their hearts, Lord,"
She prayed.

Expecting instantaneous results,
She stepped forward
Charmingly
And sensed the piano string
Strain under her weight.

The wind quietly
Held its breath
And watched her take
Another daring step.

Suddenly, the music string
Snapped out of the sky
In an unceremonious twang
Releasing the woman from the tension.

As she effortlessly plummeted,
The woman looked down
And muttered to God
"I wonder where I will land this time?"

Nellie McClung

One by one
Each page falls
Gently to earth.
Slow as time,
A Millennia of generations.

Each paragraph,
Each chapter
Compresses together.
The paper forms shale;
The ink forms oil.

Everyday I watch
The pages fall from the sky.
Every night I kick
Away the volumes
Piled at my feet.

Knee deep in eulogies,
I sincerely believe
That all I have to do is pray,
"Hey God.
Stop the presses, please!"

Writing-On-Stone

Where pretension
Breeds profit
And cynicism
Breeds clichés,
Just through
The swinging doors
Of a false-front bistro
Awaits the waiter
Of aristocracy.
From his elliptical tower
He watches us all
And dreams of
Gold plated cappuccino machines.
Ethical felonies override
His most secret desires
For love and sects
As he graciously
Serves you
Half-baked paradigms,
Snidely calling it
Your Economic Action Plan.

Trickle Down Theory

There was a lake on the screen
And we watched.
It was in black and white
But not that old.
Housewives cruised overhead on their ironing boards
And landed on oven grids
That divided the lake.
Young men in crew cuts,
With their hands in their trousers,
Stood by on the nearby rocky shore
By the Plymouth and just watched.
Knowing their briefcases were in the trunk of the car
And their pens were in the pockets
Of their short sleeved dress shirts,
The men hoped they wouldn't be impaled
By any hurdling perm rods and curlers.

Nobody Particular

Mercury clouds
Smelt like snow
As scores of billowing
Rusty Pintos
Reign molten
Ball bearings
Upon a thousand
Neon lit roadside
Cafes.
Push comes to Chevette
As the tiny people below
Become too costive,
And too naïve
To get out of the way.
Foolishly, they carry
Cotton umbrellas
To protect the little
Soft spots
On their heads.
They optimistically look up
To the heavens
But it is still
To soon Tercel.

To Windsor, With Love

Where there is premeditated spontaneity
There are diner poets
Who become belfry monkeys and weir wolves
In desperate attempts to expunge
The elliptical injustices
And legislative anathemas.
In the name of a dozen dead martyrs,
They arm themselves
With pens and quips
And crouch down in trenches
Made of newspapers and manifestos.
They uncap their Bics and Parkers,
Preparing to thrust them into the
Livingrooms of the nation.
But when they see the
Armoured Buzzcocks loom overhead,
They suddenly realise
That bullets hurt a lot more than pens.

Old Man River Dam Blockade

A thousand useless words
Clasped in his hands
Hundreds if disheveled memories
Plough through his weary mind

His breath exhales dust
For a broken land

He watches the periodic river
Slowly reprehend his homestead
Slipping past his fingers
And through his senses

He breathlessly buries himself
And calls it a day

Captain Palliser's Revenge

Mortal-fied blue mannequins,
Laying in disorder of importance
Are stacked neatly like cord wood.
Their frozen hands forever embracing
Nearly forgotten idols
Designated to oppose
The irrepressible exoneration
Of life.
In the name of science
Gaze into their
Dried out eye sockets
To seek the fears
Of a decaying empire.
Read their thin white lips
And discover
Nothing
In life or death
Is ever profound.
It's just unexpected.

Franklin Expedition

Shackled to his ancestral association
With buffalo poets
A young missionary pleads guilty
To unsafe sects
As witnessed by the Prairie Prophet.

During his rude awakening
The missionary's
Sentence is handed down
On a piece
Of Ultra Thin rolling paper.

Upon viewing the translucent
Horse blanket prophesy
The missionary begs for mercy
For his sentence reads
"As I have loved you, so you must love one another."

Born in Macleod

Using clichés so puzzling
That even Hubert Aquin
Would question their un-authenticity
She mixes them
With azoic metaphors
In the name of the arts

This She
-Who has no other name than She
For this poem would
Consequently become too personal-
Then imposes these seemingly
Inconspicuous axioms on vulnerable egos

Once more She
-The same She previously mentioned-
Becomes deceptively elated when egos
Pretend to misunderstand simple existence
And collectively attempt to propagate
Their placebo elixir as art

The Diner Poet's Ex-girlfriend

In street side cafes,
Empty truck stops,
And all across
This livingroom nation,
Local diner poets exude
Betrothed afflictions
By eliminating
All singularity
In working titles
And small town anecdotes.

Each serendipitous sip
From their chipped mugs
Seems to be the last
As they savour the warmth
Yet mourn their lost youth,
And still, they wonder why
They cannot rewrite
The Constitution
On the back of a menu
To declare their independence

Again.

Bill C-51

Evaluating his field notes,
Dr. Jon Rolo concluded
To his scientific disappointment
That his unusual symptoms
Were not just those of a common cold.
He swallowed another Tylenol
And skimmed through his diary once more.
As he sat on the desk of his
Thesis financed museum office,
The good doctor overheard a Church bus
Screech around the corner outside.
He didn't feel nauseated
From the noise,
So he shuffled through
His notes again
And to his surprise,
The autocratic doctor
Realised he was born again.

Rude Awakening

Staggering home
From an evening of oblivion
At the Marquis Tavern,
I stumbled upon a dying buffalo poet
Deliberately discarded on the street.

Perforated with slurs and lies,
He gasped for precious hope
And stared at his heaving chest.
He helplessly watched his blood dribble
Onto the sidewalk and down the gutter.

I could only drunkenly offer him
My last bottle of Lethbridge Pilsner
Concealed in my mickey pocket.
Taking a long wobbly swig, he muttered,
"I never thought it would end like this."

Suddenly, the empty stubby
Slipped from his grasp,
And clanked on the cement,
Shattering the urban silence
Just as the the poet wheezed his last.

I got up and whizzed on the white wall.
I casually watched as it dribbled
Onto the sidewalk and down the gutter.
I looked back at my bovine loving friend
And thought it should never end like this.

Royal Proclamation

From the far corners of a condemned House
The only solutions discussed
Are floating in a Chamber of admonitions
Leaking through the floorboards
To the Confederation of errors below.
Maniacs in charge boast, "Just Watch Me!"
In an era where only a few comprehend
That it is a shrinking world.
Yet people walk as far apart from each other
As possible
And the sound of a guitar
Is no longer the symbol of anything
But just another noise
Coming from a nearby room of somebody's house.

October Crisis

An Introduction to the Diner Poet

Jaybo Russell has been a writer and storyteller since the age of 7. A proud Alberta prairie boy, Jaybo has written two plays including the hit *Frank Dickens' Christmas Carol*, and the new 1950's era comedy *the Saddlemen Cometh*. Jaybo has recently penned the nonfiction *Of Mines and Men, The Unmentionable History of Drumheller Valley* to be published in 2016. He has also authored numerous short stories, and countless articles for newspapers and magazines throughout western Canada. This is his first published book of poetry.

www.ingramcontent.com/pod-product-compliance
Lightning Source LLC
Chambersburg PA
CBHW060607030426
42337CB00019B/3645